MW01609046

THE CHARM OF THE IMPOSSIBLE

BY
MARGARET SLATTERY

THE PILGRIM PRESS
BOSTON   NEW YORK   CHICAGO

THE CHARM OF THE IMPOSSIBLE

" 'THERE's no sense in going further—it's the
    end of cultivation',
So they said, and I believed it—broke my
    land and sowed my crop—
Built my barns and strung my fences in the
    little border station
Tucked away below the foothills where the
    trails run out and stop.

"Till a voice as bad as Conscience, rang in-
    terminable changes
On one everlasting Whisper day and night
    repeated—so:
'Something hidden. Go and find it. Go and
    look behind the Ranges—
Something lost behind the Ranges. Lost
    and waiting for you. Go!' "

AND men have gone. To the far-
thest corners of the earth they have
travelled in obedience to the Voice
that calls saying, "Find it, find it, find
it!"

7

Columbus heard the Voice and it rang out above all the laughter and scorn of his fellows. Having once heard it nothing could silence it. He heard it in the night time, he heard it in the day time, he could not get away from it. He followed it through Italy to Spain, to Portugal, to France, back to the palace, eager even to seize the queen's proffered jewels if thus he might obey the Voice. At last with three small ships and a convict crew he set sail. Through an unknown waste of water with his tiny ships and his handful of frightened men he followed the Voice—and found a world!

When he had whispered his dreams and hopes to his fellow men, not hearing the Voice they had answered with one accord, "Impossible—the thing is impossible." But the charm of the impossible was upon him and drew him on despite every peril until in the gray of the morning he beheld the land and knew that some day the dream would come true.

One evening a man riding on horseback along the foot-hills heard the Voice calling from the mountain tops blazing in the glory of the setting sun. "Something hidden," it said, "behind the ranges, waiting—waiting." The Voice would not leave him, it sank into his soul.

Next day when he suggested to his men that they cross the ranges they lifted their eyes to the snow capped peaks against the clear blue sky and smiled. "Impossible," they said, "the thing is impossible." But the charm

9

of the impossible burned itself into his soul. He could not silence the Voice, so he followed it and one day, flushed with victory and triumphant, he stood on the other side of the ranges and looking down upon a broad, limitless expanse of blue waters murmured —"Pacific."

There is no mountain in all the world so high but that some man has heard the Voice from its summit calling to him with irresistible power. Wooed by the charm of the impossible, man after man has scaled sheer walls of rock, crept over rivers of ice, crawled along deep canyon ledges until at last, in the cold thin air and the dead silence of the upper-world he has stood—the impossible realized and possible.

10

There is no desert so desolate but that to some soul its white, glittering sands have called. And although the gaunt cacti, fantastic and weird, have pointed their fingers in warning, crying "impossible," yet the charm of the impossible has cast its spell and through the scorching heat and burning thirst men have crossed, seeking the hidden thing.

When the Voice has called from the sea, men have launched their tiny boats and their huge liners; down into its impossible depths they have sent their divers and sub-marine boats, and in the midst of tossing billows have laid their cables to tie the nations together.

When the Voice has called from great rivers, over them men have stretched their bridges; then captured the currents and fastened them to a thousand wheels; then under the mighty stream hurrying on to the sea have buried the tubes through which crowded trains rush men on to new tasks and endeavors.

When the Voice has called from the mountains, men have built their railroads up to incredible summits, and dropped their shafts down to unthinkable depths.

From the intangible, invisible air the Voice has called, and while the world scoffed, men raised a pole and from its magic top flashed dots and dashes to the keyboard of a ship scores of miles away at sea, to send her hurrying on her mission to save her sister ship struggling vainly with wind and wave.

Now the Voice calls again, and while men hold their breath in astonishment, a fellow man wooed by the charm rises higher and higher in the sky, circles about and while they watch with tense and eager faces, he flies away and away until, a mere speck, he fades out of sight on the horizon.

The charm of the impossible—nothing can resist its power!

Today the Voice calls again. Still there is "something hidden—lost—waiting."

The Voice comes, not only from the deep recesses of great mountains, the bosom of the ocean, the desolate desert, but from the throbbing heart of humanity. And men are hearing the call. The charm has fallen upon them and the desire to accomplish the impossible burns in their souls.

" 'Something hidden—waiting' " says the Voice. The nations are large, not great; men are rich, not happy; prosperous, not fine. Greed and need dwell side by side. Prodigality and dire poverty walk the same street. True culture and false display, refinement and vulgarity meet face to face. Men do not understand one another, are not fair to one another, do not love one another.

Something is indeed hidden behind the ranges and men are beginning to go and look for it. They are going to the bottom of things, persistently striving to understand.

THE IMPOSSIBLE

"What is it?" they are asking, "that mankind has missed?" "What is the real explanation of the breaches between man and man?" "The deep hunger, the great lack—what is it?"

And from behind the ranges of social and economic difficulties the Voice has replied—"Men lack the Spirit of Brotherhood. Go and look —it is lost—waiting for you. Go!"

Men are going. All sorts and conditions of men, suddenly as one, they have heard the Voice, felt the call and have started on the long search for the Spirit of Brotherhood.

And multitudes deride and hundreds scoffingly say, "the Spirit of Brotherhood would mean Utopia, and Utopia is impossible;" yet their words are not strong enough to break the

15

charm of the impossible which has fallen upon the heart of man.

And so a great scientist who long has blest mankind gives to the world of humble men blocks of cement with which they may build for themselves comfortable, decent homes in which they need not be ashamed to live.

So a rich woman, brought up in luxury and selfishness, suddenly feeling the charm of the impossible, tears down the dirty, wretched rookeries for which men have paid her three-fourths of their hard-earned wages that they might have shelter for their families, and in their stead erects clean apartments where sunshine may at least creep in, fresh, life-giving air find its way, and little children have room enough to be good.

16

Then her sister leaves in the early morning her beautiful home with its comfort and shelter, to stand on the street corner in the chilling wind with a humble girl of the shops, to give her courage in her struggle for a living wage. The pale face of the working girl kindles with hope as she catches a glimpse of this powerful ally come to her aid.

Next, the charm falls upon the heart of a lawyer. A lawyer with "a future" if he will take it. But he hears the "voice as bad as conscience" that will not let him go. He starts his fight, sounds out the appeal wrung from a heart torn by the *facts* that stare him in the face. The power of evil fails, he wins the judgeship, the juvenile court with all that it means, is born. The impossible has become possible and still the Voice calls.

Now it speaks to officials in the public school, and poor, white-faced children, too anæmic to work, too tired to learn, too hungry to think, are given food, placed in warm bags, wrapped in sweaters and caps, are taken from ill-ventilated, overcrowded school-rooms out into the sunshine. A year passes; two years, and, strong and well, they are restored to society.

Now it speaks to a keen, strong man who catches a glimpse of the toiling childhood of the world as it hurries away in the chill of the early morning to the glass factory, the cotton mill, the coal breaker. "The helpless child of your brother man," says the Voice, "wakened from sleep so sadly needed, sent out to the long day's toil while your sheltered ones, with sweet eyes shut tight, wait their mother's kiss to waken them to another happy day."

The Voice hurts, it calls in unmistakable tones, the charm of the impossible falls upon another heart and a new seeker of the Spirit of Brotherhood starts on his journey.

In a strange place the charm falls now. It comes to a politician in a city in the hills, the boss, the leader of the ring, the man whose word is law, who has filled his purse with the coins taken one by one from the hand of his brother man. He hears the Voice, day and night. He cannot escape, he breaks with the ring, he speaks to the crowd in words of passion and power. He says that he is for justice and pure government, that he is the poor man's friend, has washed his hands and is free from the moneyed powers. He pleads with them to believe him, appeals for help to crush the evil he knows better than they. Astonished, they listen—the charm is upon him, he will yet find the hidden thing.

Again the Voice calls. This time to a young man just graduated from college. "A talented fellow," the world calls him. Practical, too, he is, sane and well-balanced. He has a fine family record, wealth, social position, everything, and he goes to the South Sea Islands to throw it all away on wild, barbaric tribes of strange, brown-skinned men.

But he has heard the Voice and behind the ranges he must go to find the Spirit of Brotherhood. If behind the ranges means to islands of the sea, it does not matter to him.

"You cannot help these men," his friends say; "let them alone, they are better off as they are. One man can do nothing on a low lying island, sleeping under a tropical sky. They will take your life; your plans are impossible dreams." Yet the look upon his face as he answers, silences them all. He must go; nothing can keep him; he has felt the charm.

Buried in the shadow of huge buildings filled with toiling thousands, lives another who has felt the charm. She might live under the cool shade of wide spreading trees in the quiet beauty of the country. But the Voice says, "No," and so she lives out her practical, helpful, sensible life in the midst of the roar and din of the city streets; amidst the clash of things that dull men's souls. "What can she do?" ask the scores who do not understand. "The task is impossible." But while they protest she discovers a new world!

Again the Voice speaks and the answer means a young physician embarking for a leper colony to bring comfort and hope to the most awful sufferers among men.

Again, and the answer sends a strong man filled with the love of congenial surroundings, home, friends, wife and child, away into the silence of the forest. Sends him tramping through deep snows, in the bitter chill of loneliness, to the very heart of the deep woods to find his brothers, losing their manhood in the temptations of the logger's camp.

It speaks yet again and finds answer in the heart of a Russian nobleman who feels the charm, attempts the impossible, loses his life and is content in the knowledge that others have gained courage through him, and will press on in the search for the hidden thing.

Once more the Voice calls and finds simultaneous answer in the hearts of an oppressed and down-trodden peasantry that rises as one man and cries, "We will be heard—give us our liberty, our birthright—we are men!"

And while the sword of power

hushes for a time the eager cry, the
Voice speaks on in

" * * one everlasting Whisper day and
   night repeated—so:
'Something hidden. Go and find it. Go
   and look behind the Ranges—
Something lost behind the Ranges. Lost
   and waiting for you. Go!' "

Every now and then, as the centuries have passed, the church as a
whole has felt the charm, has heard
the Voice, has looked behind the
ranges, ofttimes paying for that look
in persecution, trial and death. Then
for long periods of time the church
has lost the Voice; has rested "where
the trails run out and stop"; has been
content with beautiful buildings, wonderful windows, soft lights, marvel-
ous music, helpful ritual, and words
of counsel, exhortation and love.

Again, for long periods of time the church has been content to say its prayers in words, not deeds; has spent its precious days in vain discussions of pitiful phrases, while jealousy, self-satisfaction and narrowing bigotry have crept into the hearts of its people.

Then once more the Voice that has been calling, is suddenly heard. The charm falls once more over the hearts of the church and a great unrest stirs its soul.

In such a time the church finds itself today. It feels the great unrest, it sees the ranges, it hears the Voice calling with an insistence never known before. The "something hidden" tempts to new effort, the "go and find it" turns burning words of prayer into deeds that comfort, uplift and bless.

Wooed by the charm the church appeals to the world. "Men, men, O men! let us help!" it cries. "We care. Give us a chance. Give us the *facts*. Help us to understand."

At first no answer comes. Men hold aloof in distrust. Then here and there they believe in the sincerity of the cry, and slowly, slowly, both rich and poor, those in the church and those outside, open their hearts. At first in scornful, bitter words of protest the explanations come. Hot words of passion, unfair accusations, words born of deep wrongs long endured, burst forth. Behind the words lie the facts. They are hard to get, but gradually the great, bare, awful fact underlying it all stands forth for honest eyes to see—men are not brothers and they do not want to be. Under the heel of the most powerful monster hell has yet brought forth, the Spirit of Brotherhood lies weakly struggling. The name of the monster is Greed, personal Greed—and when the church sees him in all his horrible strength she too says for the moment—"The task is impossible. It is the asymptote. We cannot achieve it."

But the Voice has been heard. Day and night it is repeated. The charm has fallen upon the church and it cannot let the monster go. Already he is tormented. Here and there a muscle weakens and the end of his rule is sure. It will only take time,—time enough to educate and equip an enemy sufficiently strong to meet him and in a fair fight rob him of his power.

27

With a new zeal the church has turned to the task of equipping that enemy. His name is Character, and the church asks the assistance of *every man* in her efforts to make him pure, true and fearless, that he may be able to stand.

She hopes to equip him by means of two powerful agents—instruction and inspiration. It was by inspiration and instruction her Lord chose to equip the world with new power and to save it from itself. Neither alone was sufficient for the task.

Instruction and inspiration are both needed. He proved it.

He loved the crowd! In the street, at the feast, at the wedding, in the temple, anywhere, he loved to mingle with men, telling his wonderful stories,

28

asking his penetrating questions, healing the sick, encouraging the weak and bringing sinners to repentance. He loved to inspire the crowd, to send them away with new dreams, hopes and desires.

But when he would found a new religion, give to the world the compassionate Father in heaven, teach the new commandment that men love the Lord their God with all their hearts and their neighbors as themselves, he did not trust these things to the crowd, not even to the inspired crowd, stirred by his words and shouting "Hosanna" to his name.

No, he *taught* his new religion. By the slower method of instruction, day after day he carefully inculcated the new principles of living, explained the stories, performed miracles. The twelve special pupils he chose to instruct were manly men, men of elemental power and passion, quick to respond, slow to understand—and yet only one failed him.

The church is catching a new glimpse of the significance of his method. Here men have been inspired, not taught; there taught, not inspired. Here men have been stirred to action but not taught how to act; there instructed as to how, and left without the consuming desire to put their knowledge into everyday life.

Perhaps the fact that the church has seen with a new vision the method of Jesus, reveals itself more clearly in the Sunday school than in any other department of its work.

There it attempts the task of religious education and instruction, and there it inspires child, youth and man, and gives to each an incentive for action.

The task of even attempting religious instruction under conditions existing today is a tremendous one.

Men of all creeds and of none have agreed that religious instruction must be given. But the problem of how and by whom they have left to others for solution. Some say it must be given by the home and the home does not accept the task—sometimes because it will not, often because it cannot.

Some say, give the task to the school, but the public school cannot accept it. It can teach morals. It has taught morals, and is giving moral education more fully today than ever before. All that it might do in this line it does not yet realize, for its leaders have not yet heard the Voice nor felt the charm. But religion as such it cannot teach. The moment one begins to teach religion he stimulates thought. Thinking means questioning, and if one questions he must be answered. The church has not agreed as to the answer, and religion has not found universal phrases by which it may express itself. Until men agree and universal phrases are found, religion as such cannot be taught in a school which is public, which belongs to all alike, and in which men of all creeds and no creed have equal rights.

THE IMPOSSIBLE

The task, then, of religious instruction and inspiration falls upon the church and it meets the task with its school held for one short hour one day in the week. In that hour it must instruct and inspire all degrees of intelligence from the baby of three in the kindergarten, to the man of maturity in the adult department.

It must attempt this task with an ordinary and purely voluntary teaching force and with pupils who may attend or not as they please.

When men look at the task thoughtfully and intelligently with a broad comprehension of what it implies, it is no wonder they cry, "Impossible—the task is impossible."

But the charm has fallen upon a thousand hearts and men hear the

Voice more clearly every day. It calls them to attempt the impossible as truly as it ever called from mountain peak, ocean, or air.

And at once as if by some common, irresistible impulse men have responded to the call.

Around the need and the work a definite literature has sprung into existence, and keen-minded men are every day writing the results of thoughtful investigation and study.

Other men have plunged into the work of organization with results that have astonished even the most hopeful. Earnest, intelligent study and wise experiments have evolved an agency for the building of character whose power the future will reveal. Into the hands of thousands of men of organized classes has been put the Book which no man can read without thinking, and whose words no man can study long and not see his brother, know his brother's need and be convinced of his own duty.

The *fact,* that on a single Sunday fifty thousand men face for an hour the significant words, "Whoso hath the world's goods, and beholdeth his brother in need, and shutteth up his compassion from him, how doth the love of God abide in him?" means hope to those who have heard the Voice and felt the charm. It turns courageously to the task of equipping its young men and women for the fight.

Last Sunday fifty strong, sane, liberty-loving young men, slaves only to the temptations of passion and sin, sat down together to discuss, "Has religion really anything to offer which will help a man in the hour of temptation?" and listened to half a dozen young fellows like themselves who frankly testified that it had, explained what it had done and appealed to them to put it to the test. The fact that such a class could meet means something to those who see the summit of the distant ranges behind which something lies hidden, waiting.

Last week on a single morning, ten classes met simultaneously, and will meet every week in ten homes of wealth and fashion in a single city, to study for one hour with open Bibles, the principles of Jesus and how they may be applied to the life of every day. Those who have felt the charm, though the world shout, "The task is impossible," take courage in the presence of a fact like this.

The fact that organized classes of college men, business men, mechanics and artisans are by the score taking up seriously the study of that Book and the vital questions it inspires, are striving with all the strength of their manhood to understand it and each other, has a meaning to those who have heard the Voice.

But the Sunday school has not been content to seek only the mature men who have lived awhile in the world, seen its need and felt its temptations. Not alone with the young men and young women has the task been accepted and attempted. Inspired by the Voice, men and women have turned their attention to the most vital part of the whole problem —the boys and the girls in their teens, seeking ideals, trying to find themselves, swept away by the temptations of the street and the thousand temptations that spring up in their own complex beings. The boys and girls weakened by over-indulgence or crippled by dwarfing poverty—men and women alike are accepting the tremendous task of attempting to understand them and to supply their needs; to give them a religion which will satisfy their hunger and strengthen them to be good, while at the same time it supplies motive for service and gives instruction that the service may be real, well-balanced and sane.

The Sunday school is attempting,

as never before, to point them to men and women who are worth while, that their faith in life and men may be kept pure and strong. It points to a Florence Nightingale and says, "Women are like that. Womanhood is capable of that." It points to a simple girl who, single-handed and alone, takes up the task of supporting mother and younger children and through the hard, toiling years makes no murmur but lives her unseen, heroic life. "A girl can be like that," it says. It points to a great specialist spending day after day in the laboratory toiling unremittingly to understand, to find the cause of some great ill that he may save his fellows. No thought of danger can move him, no amount of self-sacrifice daunts him. There he

39

stands until one day the disease seizes him and he dies, passing on the knowledge so dearly bought to aid a fellow hero in his search for truth. "Men are like that," it says.

It points to a mechanic as he stands hidden away in the stifling smoke of a burning ship, keeping the engines at work though the fire creeps nearer and all physical nature cries to him to escape. There he stands until the ship touches shore and he dies while his fellow men above him are taken to safety. "Men are like that," it teaches.

It reveals the man as he holds himself steady in the hour of awful test when he may sign his name, simply his name, and feel in his hand the money which will bring to his loved ones the comforts for which they suffer. *Yet he will not sign his name.* "Men are like that."

Slowly, under such instructions, there creep into the souls of the boys and girls admiration and love for their fellow men which, with the years, may grow into something of that compassion which sent the Christ to Calvary to die that humanity might know what love means. And those who see the response of the boys and girls in their teens to such teachings of life and love rejoice that at last the Voice calling so long is beginning to be heard.

For years past the power of the charm has sent intelligent workers to the ten and twelve-year-old children, with music and lessons, stories and inspiration adapted to their needs. And longer still the little ones of six or eight have been led along sane and natural highways to the door of truth and tiny babies' feet have been guided to the Father's heart. Even to the cradle in the home the charm has drawn women, until fathers and mothers who had forgotten religion, have felt once more its power and heard its call.

Thus far the Voice has led. The teaching force has felt its power, responded to its calls. The simple fact that thousands of dollars are being paid gladly each year to leaders who shall guide the teachers in their search for knowledge of truth and ways by which it may be imparted, the simple fact that thousands of men and women are setting aside time and money to take courses of study, to read books, to take tests that they may be able more intelligently to give religious instruction and more surely and deeply inspire their pupils to be their best, to follow the Christ in *obedience* and love, means to those who have eyes to see, that the charm is increasing its power.

The Sunday school is one agency, perhaps the dynamic and potential agency, at work today; for it is intelligently inspiring the souls of men and women, young and old, and endeavoring to instruct them definitely in the things that make for character. It is at work in a large way with an organization made up of business men, theologians, students of the mind and of the heart. As an organization it is far reaching and it spares neither time nor money in its efforts to put in the hands of the workers in the individual schools the best methods, material and equipment it can discover. But this is not enough. Not here is the task complete. Not here may we sit down to rest assured that the Spirit of Brotherhood through the Sunday school will find its way into the world.

The Sunday school is not enough, for on the Sabbath day, even while teaching a class, one may hear the steady tramp of the scores of feet that pass the church, that give no thought to its school or its Bible and but little to its God. The world is so large, the time is so short and character cannot be made in a day. Out in the world where things are hard, where evils press and where character, weakened and ruined, struggles to regain control, the Voice, undaunted, calls. Here is "something hidden, waiting. Go," it says. And men hearing the words start their constructive work and their work of reform. Playgrounds and clean places of recreation and amusement spring up to do their blessed work of prevention, while rescue homes shelter the forlorn sixteen year old girl, who, lost in the puzzling whirl of life she does not understand, now cries aloud in her agony the pitiful words, which once heard can never be forgotten, "Let me die, I can never, never be good again, never, never." And, her cry at last heard, men spring to action to save her sisters. And as the facts, cold, hard facts, untinged by imagination, slowly appear, the burning desire for reform stirs scores of other hearts.

The Voice is heard and men of sterling character begin their work—the most wonderful and telling of all the varied work of man—the work of creating public sentiment. The church speaks, the school speaks, the press speaks, the honest rich and the honest poor speak, decent men of every walk in life speak. Public sentiment is aroused, men get together and seize the sword that makes the monster Greed tremble as he sees the mighty Sword of the Law turned in behalf of the weaker brother. In the power of the law the monster loosens his hold. Trembling, the Spirit of Brotherhood rises from the ground, stands upon its feet, gains strength, then points here and there over the world calling, "Go! go! the work has but begun. Your brothers! See! See!"

Thus far the Voice has led. But the Spirit of Brotherhood is weak, his voice is faint from the struggle. He cannot as yet be heard by ears closed by the roar and din of traffic, nor answered by hearts palpitating with desire for personal gain and the possession of things.

The Spirit of Brotherhood is weak but not cowardly; faint, but not fearful. His Voice, though heard only in comparatively small circles, here and there in the world, is clear and unmistakable and *he* feels the power of the charm.

47

But a few weeks past, he spoke to a group of women to whom it was reported that in certain stores in their city young girls, immature, in their early teens, received such a mere pittance for their long hours of work that only a ten cent luncheon was possible for the most prosperous among them, and the others, obliged to save the ten cents for the street care fare, went without luncheon or brought from home, wrapped in paper, crackers and bread and ate it hurriedly in the only place provided for them, a dark, narrow hall where it was impossible to sit down and where the polluted, poisoned air made it hard to stay even for a moment.

Time was, when such women would have listened to the story and dismissed it as having nothing to do with them or with their daughters. That time is past. They listened, they investigated, they found it all true and even more than they had heard. They acted. The girls now have a small, clean lunch room where the fresh air may give them a chance to regain a little of the strength they lose in the deadening atmosphere of the crowded store. The relief upon their faces as they eat and rest and talk is good to see.

But that is not all. Those women whom once the condition of such girls could not concern have gone deeper and some day they will speak with the power of the law behind them, and they will be heard.

Hardly a month ago a merchant

from whose store a bicycle was stolen faced the guilty boy in the children's court. The boy's face was pale, hard, defiant. With the kind, encouraging questions of the judge the face softened, slowly the hardened criminal disappeared and a sinning child stood in his stead. Yes, he had meant to scrape the wheel, paint it over and sell it. He needed the money—yes, his brother was so sick he couldn't sit up. Three weeks ago he lost his job. They must have food. Yes, another boy had told him it was a good way. The story told so reluctantly, told without emotion as if such things must be, went on until the merchant asked for probation for the prisoner. It was proven when he went out to get the facts. Every statement was true. In the cellar was the knife and the can of paint. On the fourth floor, on a wretched cot lay the older brother, a boy in years, but a man in experience and suffering. Each morning, he said, he tried to go to work. He couldn't. No matter how hard he tried, he could not walk. It was plainly evident he never would go to work again. The mother was there washing—just as the boy had said, the younger children helping with the work. The picture the judge had drawn from him was there—a fact. It had been so different three years ago, the mother said, before their father died. He was a good man. He had been killed in the shop—a belt slipped. They had not put on the guard. The company had been kind;

they had buried him and given a hundred dollars. She too, spoke without apparent feeling, as do those who have learned to endure.

The merchant went down the stairs out into the sunshine, pushed his way along the sidewalk crowded with noisy children, thinking of a thousand things, but most of all of the white-faced lad in the court-room. "Something is wrong," he said to himself, "that all this can be." Later, he said it to his partner and added, "Boys like him ought to have a fair chance; they haven't it. They need friends like you and me." "What can we do? Sin and poverty have existed since the world began. That we can remedy it is a foolish notion, an impossible task. There are letters awaiting your

52

attention." He picked up the letters, but before opening them turned once more to his partner and said, "Men have tunnelled under the sea. They have learned to fly—surely they can solve a problem like this. There must be a way."

The Voice had called, the charm had gripped him and one more was added that day to the host of individuals seeking the welfare of their fellows.

It is a great day in which to be alive. The world is filled with effort, organized and unorganized, expressed in club, society, school and church, but joined in one purpose—to create a higher type of character, a more sensitive community conscience, a better public sentiment—that the Spirit of

Brotherhood may have a chance in solving the complex problems of humanity.

The time has come when more than one Columbus stands on the shore of unknown seas determined to make the venture—more than one Marconi experiments with invisible ether waves with confidence that some time through empty, unresponsive space the answer will come. But many grow weary in the struggle with great odds, push aside the task and say, "I am tired."

"Tired? Well, what of that—
  Didst fancy life was spent on beds of ease
Fluttering the rose leaves
  Scattered by the breeze?
Come, rouse thee, work
  While it is called today.
Tired? Arise, go forth
  Upon thy way."

THE IMPOSSIBLE

The seemingly impossible is only difficult, *hard*.

"Hard? Well, what of that?
  Didst fancy life one summer holiday
With lessons naught to learn
  And naught but play?
Go, get thee to the task!
  Conquer or die—
Truth must be learned;
  Learn it then patiently."

The Spirit of Brotherhood—it is the Spirit of Christ. For centuries in a thousand tongues, to the little child in the morning, to the youth in the heat of the day, to the old in the twilight, from behind the ranges it has called, "Something hidden—lost— waiting for *you*." Go—follow the Christ, and find it.

CPSIA information can be obtained
at www.ICGtesting.com
Printed in the USA
LVHW080335070323
741055LV00005B/702